D0560739

Dedication

*This book is dedicated to
members of the Catholic community
who in faith participated in the
research and development of this
sizable undertaking.
Many people contributed helpful
suggestions to portions of this text.
Our gratitude is expressed to all of
them collectively.*

*Special thanks go to those who
persistently encouraged the
creation of this Communion Book.
In particular, we wish to thank:
J.G., C.N., J.D., P.W. and D.M.*

*Thanks go to the children,
Fr. Bill Kernan and the supportive
community of St. Francis of
Assisi Parish.*

Prayer Before A Crucifix

Look down on me, good and gentle Jesus. Make my soul strong in faith, hope and love. Make me really sorry for my sins so I will never sin again.

I am sad when I see the wounds on your hands and feet, and think of the words of your prophet, David: "They have pierced my hands and feet, they have hurt all my bones."

A Record of My First Eucharist

My Name Is

_____

My Parents Are

_____

I Live at

_____

_____

**I received
My First
Holy Communion
in the Parish of**

_____

in the City of

_____

on the _____ **Day**

of _____

in _____

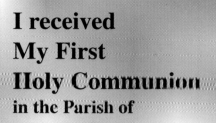

"Let the children come to me, and do not prevent them; for the kingdom of heaven belongs to such as these." After he placed his hands on them, he went away. re: Matt 19:14-15

My Mass and Holy Communion Book

A *New* Mass and Prayer Book for Today's Catholic Community

*Illustrations were created specifically for
My Mass and Holy Communion Book
by pastelist Teresa Biernacki, USA.*

**Published by
Devon Trading Corporation
New Jersey**

Nihil Obstat & Imprimatur

I have concluded that the materials
presented in this work are free of
doctrinal or moral errors.

Bernadeane Carr, STL
Censor Librorum
October 13, 1995

In accord with 1983 CIC 827, permission
to publish this work is hereby granted.

† Robert H. Brom
Bishop of San Diego
October 16, 1995

ISBN	1-888765-10-0	Traditional	Girl
ISBN	1-888765-11-9	Traditional	Boy

My Mass and Holy Communion Book

9

Boys and Girls:

This is your very own Mass and Communion book. You can use it in Church and at home for a long time.

This book can help you to understand the Mass. The beautiful pictures show what the priest is doing at the altar. What to do and what to say during Mass is explained.

Your book is full of special sections. In the prayer section, you can read your prayers until you learn them. There is a place for you to add your favorite sayings or other prayers.

The Rosary tells about the life of Jesus and his family. The words about Jesus are from the Bible.

The Stations of the Cross show how much Jesus loved us.

Being a Catholic means following Jesus and learning what Jesus teaches us. When we receive the Sacraments we follow Jesus. He wants all of us to obey the Commandments and to live the Beatitudes.

May you continue to grow in the Way of Jesus who is Truth and Life — *Peace be to you*.

Vessels
Used During
the Mass

Du   uring the Mass special vessels
                         are used to hold the water, wine
                         and bread. Vessels are made
from different materials.

The sacred vessels used during the Mass are
the Chalice and Paten. Because they hold
Jesus' Body and Blood, they are blessed.
They are made of very precious materials to
signify how special the celebration of the
Mass is. Silver and gold as well as other
precious materials may be used according
to tradition.

CHALICE — *Or Cup, is used to hold the wine which becomes the Blood of Jesus. It is made of gold, silver or other precious materials.*

PATEN — *Or Plate, is used to hold the bread which becomes the Body of Jesus. A Bowl may also be used.*

INTRODUCTION
TO THE
HOLY MASS

The Mass is the center of our worship of God. Together with the priest, our family, friends and neighbors, we celebrate the sacrifice of Jesus Christ. During the Mass, God speaks to us in the Bible readings and the priest's teachings. We pray, sing and praise the Father, Son and Holy Spirit.

Jesus is with us in many ways. In the Mass, he is especially with us in the

Eucharistic food. Jesus offers himself to our heavenly Father for everyone. We offer ourselves with Jesus to our heavenly Father.

Under the appearances of bread and wine, Jesus becomes food for our souls as the priest says the words, *"This is my Body. This is my Blood."* At Mass, everyone joins in the celebration of thanksgiving and love *through Jesus, with Jesus and in Jesus.*

ORDER OF THE HOLY MASS

INTRODUCTORY RITES

We Stand

As a Catholic community, we celebrate the Holy Sacrifice of the Mass.

ENTRANCE

If not sung, it is recited by all or by some of the people.

←THE ENTRANCE PROCESSION is led by altar servers. Next, the lector carries the Lectionary from which the Word of God is read to the people, followed by the priest. When the priest reaches the altar he kisses it in reverence because the altar is the symbol of Christ. Then he says the greeting.

GREETING

PRIEST: In the name of the Father, and of the Son, and of the Holy Spirit.

PEOPLE: Amen.

PRIEST: The grace of our Lord Jesus Christ and the love of God and the fellowship of the Holy Spirit be with you all.

PEOPLE: And also with you.

Or the priest says other prayers like,
PRIEST: The grace and peace of God our Father and the Lord Jesus Christ be with you.

PEOPLE: And also with you.

*When the Rite of Blessing and Sprinkling
of Holy Water is celebrated, it takes
the place of the Penitential Rite — the
Confiteor and the Kyrie are not said.*

PENITENTIAL RITE

PRIEST: As we prepare to celebrate
the mystery of Christ's love, let us
acknowledge our failures and ask
the Lord for pardon and strength.
  (or similar words)
PEOPLE: And also with you.

PRIEST AND PEOPLE:
I confess to almighty God,
and to you, my brothers and sisters,
that I have sinned through my own fault
 (They strike their breast)
in my thoughts and in my words,
in what I have done,
and in what I have failed to do;

and I ask blessed Mary, ever virgin,
all the angels and saints,
and you, my brothers and sisters,
to pray for me to the Lord our God.

The priest says the absolution.

PRIEST: May almighty God have
mercy on us,
forgive us our sins,
and bring us to everlasting life.

PEOPLE: Amen.

KYRIE

PRIEST: Lord have mercy.

PEOPLE: Lord have mercy.

PRIEST: Christ have mercy.

PEOPLE: Christ have mercy.

PRIEST: Lord have mercy.

PEOPLE: Lord have mercy.

GLORIA

The Gloria is not said during Lent.

PRIEST AND PEOPLE:

Glory to God in the highest,
  and peace to his people on earth.

Lord God, heavenly King,
almighty God and Father,
  we worship you, we give you thanks,
  we praise you for your glory.

Lord Jesus Christ, only Son of the
  Father,
Lord God, Lamb of God,
you take away the sin of the world:
  have mercy on us;
you are seated at the right hand of
  the Father: receive our prayer.

For you alone are the Holy One,
you alone are the Lord,
you alone are the Most High,
  Jesus Christ,
  with the Holy Spirit,
  in the glory of God the Father.   Amen.

OPENING PRAYER

PRIEST: Let us pray.

The priest and people pray silently. Then the priest says the opening prayer and concludes:

PRIEST: ...for ever and ever.

PEOPLE: Amen.

LITURGY OF THE WORD

We Sit

God speaks to us through readings from the Bible in the Old Testament and New Testament.

FIRST READING

Ending the reading:

READER: The word of the Lord.
PEOPLE: Thanks be to God.

RESPONSORIAL PSALM

We repeat the response sung or said by the reader. After each verse, we repeat the response.

SECOND READING

At the end:

READER: The word of the Lord.
PEOPLE: Thanks be to God.

GOSPEL ACCLAMATION

After the reader or choir sings alleluia,
we sing:

PEOPLE: ALLELUIA!

The alleluia or other chant may be
omitted if not sung.
The alleluia is not sung during Lent.

GOSPEL

DEACON OR PRIEST: The Lord
be with you.

PEOPLE: And also with you.

DEACON OR PRIEST: A reading
from the holy gospel according to N–.

PEOPLE: Glory to you, Lord.

At the end:

DEACON OR PRIEST: The gospel of the Lord.

PEOPLE: Praise to you, Lord Jesus Christ.

`We Sit`

HOMILY

Listening to the priest explaining the readings from the Bible helps us put God's message into practice. We learn about Jesus' life and his teachings from the Gospels. The Gospels are taken from the writings of the 4 evangelists: Matthew, Mark, Luke and John. You will find their writings in the New Testament of the Bible.

We Stand

PROFESSION OF FAITH

When we say the Creed, we believe everything God teaches us.

PEOPLE:

We believe in one God,
   the Father, the Almighty,
   maker of heaven and earth,
   of all that is seen and unseen.

We believe in one Lord, Jesus Christ,
   the only Son of God,
   eternally begotten of the Father,
   God from God, Light from Light,
   true God from true God,

begotten, not made, one in Being
    with the Father.
Through him all things were made.
For us men and for our salvation
    he came down from heaven:

All bow during these three lines:
by the power of the Holy Spirit
    he was born of the Virgin Mary,
       and became man.

For our sake he was crucified under
    Pontius Pilate;
    he suffered, died, and was buried.
On the third day he rose again
    in fulfillment of the Scriptures;
    he ascended into heaven
       and is seated at the right hand of
          the Father.
He will come again in glory to judge

the living and the dead,
   and his kingdom will have no end.

We believe in the Holy Spirit,
   the Lord, the giver of life,
who proceeds from the Father and
   the Son.
With the Father and the Son he is
   worshipped and glorified.
He has spoken through the Prophets.
We believe in one holy catholic and
   apostolic Church.
We acknowledge one baptism for
   the forgiveness of sins.
We look for the resurrection of
   the dead,
      and the life of the world to come.
         Amen.

*The Apostles' Creed may be said instead,
see page 67.*

GENERAL INTERCESSIONS

We unite with our community, the entire Church and all people, to pray for their needs. After each intention is said, we say:

PEOPLE: Lord hear our prayer.

(or similar words)

The priest ends with a concluding prayer. We say:

PEOPLE: Amen.

We Sit

LITURGY OF THE EUCHARIST

As in the early days of the Church, we bring our gifts to the altar. Our offerings of bread and wine are presented. The priest places the bread and wine on the altar as the preparation song is sung. →

Preparation of the Bread

Holding the bread slightly above the altar, the priest says:

PRIEST: Blessed are you, Lord,
God of all creation.
Through your goodness we
have this bread to offer,
which earth has given and
human hands have made.
It will become for us
the bread of life.

PEOPLE: Blessed be God for ever.

Preparation of the Wine

Holding the wine slightly above the altar, the priest says:

PRIEST: Blessed are you, Lord,

God of all creation.

Through your goodness we

have this wine to offer,

fruit of the vine and work

of human hands.

It will become our spiritual

drink.

PEOPLE: Blessed be God for ever.

PRAYER OVER THE GIFTS

PRIEST: Pray brethren, that our sacrifice
may be acceptable to God,
the almighty Father.

**PEOPLE: May the Lord accept
the sacrifice at your hands
for the praise and glory of his name,
for our good, and the good of all
his Church.**

`We Stand`

*The priest asks God to accept our gifts.
At the end, we say:*

PEOPLE: Amen.

EUCHARISTIC PRAYER

The priest begins an important part of the Mass, the Eucharistic Prayer.

We join in with prayers of praise and thanksgiving.

PRIEST: The Lord be with you.
PEOPLE: And also with you.

PRIEST: Lift up your hearts.
PEOPLE: We lift them up to the Lord.

PRIEST: Let us give thanks to the Lord our God.
PEOPLE: It is right to give him thanks and praise.

PREFACE

The priest continues giving God thanks and praise for saving us.

We join in with the song of the saints and angels.

ACCLAMATION

PRIEST AND PEOPLE:

Holy, holy, holy Lord, God of
power and might.
Heaven and earth are full of
your glory.
Hosanna in the highest.
Blessed is he who comes in the
name of the Lord.
Hosanna in the highest.

We Kneel

*In this part of the Eucharistic
Prayer, the priest recalls the words
of Jesus and prays for the church,*

peace and salvation. He asks the Father to accept the offerings.

He calls upon the Holy Spirit so that the gifts of bread and wine will become the Body and Blood of Jesus. The priest says the same words that Jesus spoke during the Last Supper.

Taking the bread, the priest proclaims:

PRIEST:
Take this, all of you, and eat it:
this is my body which will be
    given up for you.

THE BREAD BECOMES THE BODY OF CHRIST. Jesus is present to us in the Eucharist. Jesus gives us his own Body and Blood that we might have life everlasting.→

The priest, taking the chalice says:

PRIEST: Take this, all of you,
and drink from it:
this is the cup of my blood,
the blood of the new and
everlasting covenant.
It will be shed for you and for all
so that sins may be forgiven.
Do this in memory of me.

THE WINE BECOMES THE BLOOD OF CHRIST. We celebrate and adore Jesus present in the bread and wine.→

PRIEST: Let us proclaim the
mystery of faith.

**PEOPLE: Christ has died, Christ
is risen, Christ will come again.**
(Other words may be used.)

Next we remember the life, death and resurrection of Jesus. We pray in our hearts as the priest prays for members of our Church — those who are dead, and the Communion of Saints.

At the end of the priest's prayer, we say "The Great Amen"→

PRIEST:
Through him,
with him,
in him,
in the unity of the Holy Spirit,
all glory and honor is yours,
almighty Father,
for ever and ever.

PEOPLE: Amen.

COMMUNION RITE

THE LORD'S PRAYER

PRIEST: Let us pray with confidence to the Father in the words our Savior gave us.

We Stand

PRIEST AND PEOPLE:

Our Father, who art in heaven, hallowed be thy name; thy kingdom come;

thy will be done on
earth as it is in heaven.

Give us this day our
daily bread;
and forgive us our
trespasses
as we forgive those
who trespass against us;
and lead us not into
temptation,
but deliver us from evil.

PRIEST:
Deliver us, Lord, from every evil,
and grant us peace in our day.
In your mercy keep us free from sin
and protect us from all anxiety
as we wait in joyful hope
for the coming of our Savior,
   Jesus Christ.

DOXOLOGY

PEOPLE:
**For the kingdom, the power,
   and the glory are yours,
   now and forever.**

*The Church is a community. Before
receiving Jesus, we wish each other
the peace of Christ. This is a sign
of forgiveness and being in unity
as a community.*

SIGN OF PEACE

PRIEST:
Lord Jesus Christ, you said to
        your apostles:
I leave you peace, my peace I give you.
Look not on our sins, but on the faith
        of your Church,
and grant us the peace and unity of
        your kingdom
where you live for ever and ever.

PEOPLE: Amen.

PRIEST: The peace of the Lord be
with you always.

PEOPLE: And also with you.

DEACON OR PRIEST: Let us offer
each other the sign of peace.

SIGN OF PEACE

BREAKING OF THE BREAD

We sing or say:

PEOPLE: Lamb of God, you take away the sins of the world:
> **have mercy on us.**

Lamb of God, you take away the sins of the world:
> **have mercy on us.**

Lamb of God, you take away the sins of the world:
> **grant us peace.**

*The priest breaks the host →
over the paten. He places a small piece
in the chalice, saying quietly:*

PRIEST: May this mingling of the body and blood of our Lord Jesus Christ bring eternal life to us who receive it.

We get ready to receive Jesus. We ask Jesus to keep us faithful and to never be parted from him.

COMMUNION

PRIEST: This is the Lamb of God who takes away the sins of the world.
Happy are those who are called to his supper.

PRIEST AND PEOPLE: Lord, I am not worthy to receive you, but only say the word and I shall be healed.

Quietly the priest says:

PRIEST: May the body of Christ bring me to everlasting life.
May the blood of Christ bring me to everlasting life.

We walk up to receive Jesus in Communion (See the picture on the next page). When we receive Holy Communion, the Eucharistic minister, deacon or priest says:

MINISTER, DEACON OR PRIEST: The body of Christ.
WE SAY: Amen.

MINISTER, DEACON OR PRIEST: The blood of Christ.
WE SAY: Amen.

The other way the Eucharist may be received is on the tongue.

PRAYER AFTER COMMUNION

After Communion, we pray to Jesus in our hearts.

$\rightarrow$

PRIEST: Let us pray.

The priest says the prayer after Communion. At the end, the priest says:

PRIEST: We ask this through Christ our Lord.
PEOPLE: Amen.

CONCLUDING RITE

We heard the Word of God, received Jesus in Holy Communion and prayed in unity with the Holy Spirit. Now, it is time to go out and do good works. By loving others, we show how much we love Jesus.

PRIEST: The Lord be with you.
PEOPLE: And also with you.

The priest blesses the people. →

BLESSING

PRIEST: May almighty God bless you, the Father, and the Son, † and the Holy Spirit.

PEOPLE: Amen.

DISMISSAL

DEACON OR PRIEST:
Go in peace to love and serve the Lord.

(Other words may be used. On Easter Sunday, alleluias are added.)

PEOPLE: Thanks be to God.
(We add alleluias on Easter.)

How We Live

As Catholics, we live our lives keeping in touch with God through prayer. We follow the will of God by keeping his commandments. We worship God together in community and individually.

Worship is giving honor and praise to God. Our Baptism calls us to honor God and follow Jesus. We worship God in the Mass, through the reading of the Scriptures and receiving Holy Communion. When we receive Jesus in the Eucharist, we are given the grace to live our Catholic faith and follow Jesus more completely.

Prayer

Prayer is an important part of being a Catholic. To follow Jesus and to be closer to our heavenly Father, we pray. Through prayer, we come to know God as our very own Father.

What is prayer?

Praying is talking and listening to God. Praying is a two-way conversation. Listening and talking to God are very important. That is why we need to set aside a special time to listen to God. A good time to pray is at the start of the day — before all the other things we like to do — and at the end of the day, after a full day of activities.

How do we pray?

There are many different ways to pray. We can pray by speaking from our hearts to God. We can also say prayers that come from the Bible. There are memorized prayers and group prayers, too. Prayers have many different messages. There are prayers that ask God for what we need and prayers for giving thanks. There are prayers that ask for others' needs, and prayers for forgiveness. There are prayers of sorrow, and prayers of joy. There are prayers to adore God and praise Him for everything that is holy. The greatest prayer of all is the Holy Mass.

Prayers

Say during the day, or when the need arises.

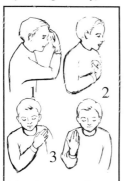

Sign of the Cross

(1) In the name of the Father,

(2) and of the Son, and of the

(3) Holy Spirit, Amen.

Morning Offering

Heavenly Father, I believe in you and hope in you. I love you above all things. Thank you for bringing me safely through the night. Today, I give myself and everything I do to you. Keep me from evil. Bless my family, friends and all those I love. In Jesus' name I pray. Amen.

Evening Prayer

Heavenly Father, thank you for this day. Thank you for our many blessings. Please forgive anything that I did knowingly or unknowingly that displeased you. Please forgive anything I did that hurt others. Father, help me to do better in following Jesus tomorrow. Bless my family and friends all through the night. In Jesus' name I pray. Amen.

Apostles' Creed

I believe in God, the Father almighty,
creator of heaven and earth.
I believe in Jesus Christ, his only Son,
  our Lord;
  He was conceived by the power of the
  Holy Spirit
    and born of the Virgin Mary.
  He suffered under Pontius Pilate,
    was crucified, died and was buried.
  He descended to the dead.
  On the third day he arose again.
  He ascended into heaven,
    and sits at the right hand of the Father.
  He will come again to judge the living and
    the dead.
I believe in the Holy Spirit,
  the holy catholic church,
  the communion of saints,
  the forgiveness of sins,
  the resurrection of the body
  and the life everlasting. Amen.

Our Father

See pages 46 & 47.

Hail Mary

Hail Mary, full of grace, the Lord is with you. Blessed are you among women, and blessed is the fruit of your womb, Jesus. Holy Mary, Mother of God, pray for us sinners, now, and at the hour of our death. Amen.

Glory to the Father

Glory to the Father, and to the Son, and to the Holy Spirit: as it was in the beginning, is now, and will be for ever. Amen.

Hail, Holy Queen

Hail, holy Queen, Mother of mercy; hail our life, our sweetness and our hope. To you do we cry, poor banished children of Eve. To you do we send up our sighs, mourning and weeping in this valley of tears. Turn then, most gracious Advocate, your eyes of mercy toward us. And after this our exile show unto us the blessed fruit of your womb, Jesus. O clement, O loving, O sweet Virgin Mary.

The Memorare

Remember, O most gracious Virgin Mary, that never was it known that anyone who fled to your protection, implored your help or sought your intercession, was left unaided. Inspired

 with this confidence, I fly to you O Virgin of virgins, my Mother; to you do I come, before you I stand, sinful and sorrowful. O Mother of the Word Incarnate, despise not my petitions, but in your mercy hear and answer me. Amen.

Prayer of Sorrow

My God,
I am sorry for my sins with all my heart.
In choosing to do wrong
and failing to do good,
I have sinned against you
whom I should love above all things.

I firmly intend, with your help,
to do penance,
to sin no more,
and to avoid whatever leads me to sin.

Our Savior Jesus Christ
suffered and died for us.
In his name, my God, have mercy.

GRACE BEFORE MEALS

Bless us, O Lord, and these your gifts,
which we are about to receive from
your goodness, through Christ our
Lord. Amen.

St. Francis of Assisi, grew up as Francesco Bernadone from 1181–1226 A.D. Francis saw the face of God in everything. He began the Franciscan religious order which spread all over the world.

Prayer of
St. Francis of Assisi

Lord, make me an instrument of your
peace.

Where there is hatred, let me sow
love;

Where there is injury, pardon;

Where there is doubt, faith;

Where there is despair, hope;

Where there is darkness, light;

And where there is sadness, joy.

O divine Master, grant that I may not
so much seek to be consoled as to
console;
to be understood as to understand;
to be loved as to love.

For it is in giving that we receive, it
is in pardoning that we are
pardoned,
and it is in dying that we are born
to eternal life.

The Rosary

The Rosary is a prayer. It was developed a long time ago. At first, the Rosary was much different. Today, we say the Rosary developed by St. Louis de Montfort in the 1700's. It is made of 15 Mysteries (150 Hail Mary beads) divided into three groups — the Joyful, Sorrowful, and Glorious Mysteries.

Praying the Rosary, we remember the mysteries in the lives of Jesus and Mary. Mary was Jesus' mother and she is our mother, too. Praying the Rosary helps us think about Jesus and how much Mary and Jesus love us.

WHEN TO PRAY THE ROSARY

The Mysteries of the Rosary are always said in the same order. The order follows Jesus' life. First the Joyful followed by the Sorrowful and Glorious Mysteries. That is why we say them throughout the week in this order:

- Pray the 5 Joyful Mysteries on Monday and Thursday.

- Pray the 5 Sorrowful Mysteries every Tuesday and Friday.

- Pray the 5 Glorious Mysteries every Wednesday, Saturday and Sunday.

How to pray the Rosary

The illustration to the right shows with which beads the Apostles' Creed, the Our Father, Hail Mary and Glory to the Father are prayed.

1. Apostles' Creed
2. Say 1 Our Father
3. Say 3 Hail Marys
4. Say 1 Glory to the Father

For each Mystery

5. Announce the Mystery and decade
6. Followed with 1 Our Father
7. Say 10 Hail Marys
8. Say 1 Glory to the Father

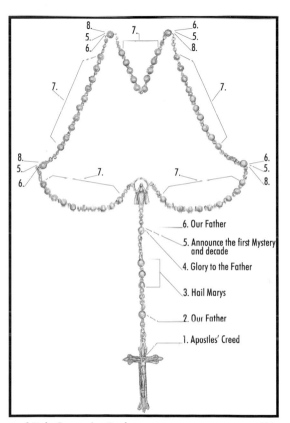

6. Our Father

5. Announce the first Mystery and decade

4. Glory to the Father

3. Hail Marys

2. Our Father

1. Apostles' Creed

The 5 Joyful Mysteries

1. The Annunciation

The angel Gabriel was sent from God to ... Mary. The angel said, "Hail, favored one! The Lord is with you. You have found favor with God. Behold, you will conceive in your womb and bear a son, and you shall name him Jesus." Mary said, "Behold, I am the handmaid of the Lord. May it be done to me according to your word." *(re: Luke 1:26-28, 30-31, 38)*

Like Mary, help me to humbly say "yes"
to God.
(Say 1 Our Father,
10 Hail Marys, 1 Glory to the Father)

2. The Visitation

Mary set out and traveled to the hill country ... she entered the house of Zechariah and greeted Elizabeth. When Elizabeth heard Mary's greeting, the infant leaped in her womb, and Elizabeth, filled with the holy Spirit, cried out... and said, "Most blessed are you among women, and blessed is the fruit of your womb." *(re: Luke 1: 39-42)*

When the Holy Spirit fills my soul, it is
God's grace and love that abound.
*(Say 1 Our Father,
10 Hail Marys, 1 Glory to the Father)*

3. The Birth of Jesus

While they (Mary and Joseph) were in Bethlehem, the time came for her to have her child, and she gave birth to her firstborn son. She wrapped him in swaddling clothes and laid him in a manger, because there was no room for them in the inn. *(re: Luke 2: 6-7)*

May I receive the grace to be poor
in spirit.
(Say 1 Our Father,
10 Hail Marys, 1 Glory to the Father)

4. The Presentation of Jesus

According to the law of Moses, they took Jesus up to Jerusalem to present him to the Lord. Now there was a man in Jerusalem whose name was Simeon. This man was righteous and devout... And when the parents brought in the child Jesus... he took him into his arms and blessed God... *(re: Luke 2:22-25, 27-28)*

Help me to be obedient like Jesus, Mary
and Joseph were to the laws of God.
*(Say 1 Our Father,
10 Hail Marys, 1 Glory to the Father)*

5. Finding Jesus in the Temple

When Jesus was twelve years old, they went up to Jerusalem according to festival custom. After they had completed its days, as they were returning, the boy Jesus remained behind in Jerusalem, but his parents did not know it. Not finding him, they returned to Jerusalem to look for him. After three days they found him in the temple, sitting in the midst of the teachers, listening to them and asking them questions, and all who heard him were astounded at his understanding and his answers... He went ... to Nazareth, and was obedient to them... And Jesus advanced (in) wisdom and age and favor before God and man. *(re: Luke 2: 42-47, 51-52)*

Lord, help me to grow in knowledge
and piety.
(Say 1 Our Father,
10 Hail Marys, 1 Glory to the Father)

The 5 Sorrowful Mysteries

1. Agony in the Garden

Jesus came with the disciples to a place called Gethsemane... and he began to feel sorrow and distress. He advanced a little and fell prostrate in prayer, saying, "My Father, if it is possible, let this cup pass from me; yet, not as I will, but as you will." *(re: Matt 26: 36, 37, 39 & Luke 22:42)*

Heavenly Father, when it is difficult
to do the right thing, help me to do
what is right.
(Say 1 Our Father,
10 Hail Marys, 1 Glory to the Father)

2. Scourging at the Pillar

They bound Jesus, led him away, and handed him over to Pilate. Pilate questioned him, "Are you the king of the Jews?" Jesus answered, "My kingdom does not belong to this world. You say I am a king. For this I was born and for this I came into the world, to testify to the truth." Then Pilate said, "I find this man not guilty. Therefore I shall have him flogged and then release him." Then Pilate took Jesus and had him scourged.

(re: Mark 15: 1, 2; John 18: 36, 37; Luke 23: 4, 16; John 19: 1)

Jesus you love us so much that you
suffered for our sins so we would
be purified.
(Say 1 Our Father,
10 Hail Marys, 1 Glory to the Father)

3. Crowning of Thorns

The soldiers led Jesus away inside the palace. They stripped off his clothes and threw a scarlet cloak about him. Weaving a crown out of thorns, they placed it on his head... and kneeling before him, they mocked him, saying, "Hail! King of the Jews!" *(re: Mark 15:16; Matt 27: 28, 29)*

Give me strength and courage to follow
you even when others hurt me and
put me down.
(Say 1 Our Father,
10 Hail Marys, 1 Glory to the Father)

4. Carrying of the Cross

Carrying the cross himself he went out to what is called the Place of the Skull.

(re: John 19:17)

Following Jesus is sometimes difficult. Jesus tells us that following him may not always feel good.

"If anyone wishes to come after me, he must deny himself and take up his cross daily and follow me."

(re: Luke 9:23)

When my cross is heavy, Lord, help me
to have patience and follow your will in
my life.
(Say 1 Our Father,
10 Hail Marys, 1 Glory to the Father)

5. The Crucifixion

When they came to the place called the Skull, they crucified him... Then Jesus said, "Father, forgive them, they know not what they do." Now one of the criminals hanging there... said, "Jesus, remember me when you come into your kingdom." ...Darkness came over the whole land until three in the afternoon because of an eclipse of the sun. Then the veil of the temple was torn down the middle. Jesus cried out in a loud voice, "Father, into your hands I commend my spirit"; and when he had said this he breathed his last.

(re: Luke 23:33-34, 39, 42, 44-46)

Jesus you sacrificed yourself for my sins
that I, and all the world, might be saved.
Help me to have true sorrow for my sins.
(Say 1 Our Father,
10 Hail Marys, 1 Glory to the Father)

The 5 Glorious Mysteries

1. The Resurrection of Jesus

At daybreak on the first day of the week they took the spices they had prepared and went to the tomb. And behold, there was a great earthquake; for an angel of the Lord descended from heaven, approached, rolled back the stone... the angel said... "Do not be afraid! I know that you are seeking Jesus the crucified. He is not here, for he has been raised just as he said. Come and see the place where he lay." *(re: Luke 24:1; Matt 28:2, 5, 6)*

Jesus help me to know the joy of your resurrection and always believe in you.
(Say 1 Our Father,
10 Hail Marys, 1 Glory to the Father)

2. The Ascension of Jesus

Then Jesus led them (out) as far as Bethany, raised his hands, and blessed them. Then Jesus... said to them, "All power in heaven and on earth has been given to me. Go therefore, and make disciples of all nations, baptizing them in the name of the Father, and of the Son, and of the holy Spirit... behold, I am with you always, until the end of the age." As he blessed them he parted from them and was taken up to heaven.

(re: Luke 24:50-51; Matt 28:18-19, 20)

Help me to share my faith and hope in you with others. Let me never be distant from you.
(Say 1 Our Father,
10 Hail Marys, 1 Glory to the Father)

3. The Descent of the Holy Spirit upon the Apostles

When the time for Pentecost was fulfilled, they were in one place together. And suddenly there came from the sky a noise like a strong driving wind.... Then there appeared to them tongues as of fire, which parted and came to rest on each one of them. And they were all filled with the holy Spirit and began to speak in different tongues, as the Spirit enabled them to proclaim ... the mighty acts of God. *(re: Acts 2:1-4, 11)*

Through the gifts of the Holy Spirit,
help me to love God and others more.
(Say 1 Our Father,
10 Hail Marys, 1 Glory to the Father)

4. The Assumption of Mary

Blessed are you, daughter, by the Most High God, above all the women on earth.

(re: Judith 13:18)

Mary, you were assumed into Heaven as a sign of our hope to also live in heaven. Because of Jesus, may I too be given eternal happiness.

**(Say 1 Our Father,
10 Hail Marys, 1 Glory to the Father)**

5. The Crowning of Mary as Queen of Heaven and Earth

A great sign appeared in the sky, a woman clothed with the sun, with the moon under her feet, and on her head a crown of twelve stars. Who is this that comes forth like the dawn, as beautiful as the moon, as resplendent as the sun?

(re: Rev. 12:1; Song of Songs, 6:10)

Mary, my queen and my mother, help me
to remain faithful to you and the will of
God.
(*Say 1 Our Father,
10 Hail Marys, 1 Glory to the Father*)

The Sacraments

Sacraments are visible signs established by Christ in which God's life is given to us. The sacraments are entrusted to the Church. They touch every important part of our Christian life of faith. At the Last Supper, Jesus gave us the Eucharist. The Eucharist is the Sacrament of Christ's Body and Blood. The Eucharist is at the center of our sacramental life.

While they were eating, Jesus took bread, said the blessing, broke it, and giving it to his disciples said, "Take and eat; this is my body." Then he took a cup, gave thanks, and gave it to them, saying, "Drink from it, all of you, for this is my blood of the covenant, which will be shed on behalf of many for the forgiveness of sins." (re: Matt 26:26-28)

The 7 Sacraments are divided into three groups.

1. Sacraments of Initiation

- Baptism
- Confirmation
- Eucharist

2. Sacraments of Healing

- Penance / Reconciliation
- Anointing of the Sick

3. Sacraments at the Service of Communion

- Holy Orders
- Matrimony

I was baptized on_____

in the Church of

_____

Restoring our Relationship with God

When we sin, it is important to reconcile ourselves with God. Through the Sacrament of Reconciliation we are forgiven. The Sacrament of Reconciliation celebrates God's love and forgiveness.

Before confessing our sins, we examine our conscience. We think about what we said or did that was wrong. Did we break one or more of the Commandments of God?

The 10 Commandments

Loving God above all things

1. *I am the Lord your God: you shall not have strange gods before me.*

    We believe in God and love God — no person or thing is more important.

2. *You shall not take the name of the Lord your God in vain.*

    We use God's name with love because it is holy.

3. *Remember to keep holy the Lord's Day.*

    We pray, go to Church and attend Mass on Sunday and holy days.

Loving our neighbor

4. *Honor your father and your mother.*

    We listen to and obey our parents and those who care for us.

5. *You shall not kill.*
   We should respect each person's life
   and dignity.

6. *You shall not commit adultery.*
   We are faithful to our loved ones.

7. *You shall not steal.*
   We must never take anything which
   does not belong to us.

8. *You shall not bear false witness against your
   neighbor.*
   We always tell the truth, and are
   careful not to gossip.

9. *You shall not covet your neighbor's wife.*
   We are thankful for those God has
   given us to love.

10. *You shall not covet your neighbor's goods.*
    We appreciate all the things God has
    given us.

(re: Exodus 20:2-17; Deuteronomy 5:6-21)

The 2 Great Commandments

hen Jesus came, he gave us 2 commandments that cover everything we must do as followers of Christ.

"You shall love the Lord, your God, with all your heart, with all your soul, and with all your mind. This is the greatest and the first commandment.

The second is like it: You shall love your neighbor as yourself."

(re: Matt 22: 37-39)

The Beatitudes

True happiness is following the teachings of Jesus.

Blessed are the poor in spirit,
for theirs is the kingdom of heaven.

Blessed are they who mourn,
for they will be comforted.

Blessed are the meek,
for they will inherit the land.

Blessed are they who hunger and thirst
for righteousness,
for they will be satisfied.

Blessed are the merciful,
for they will be shown mercy.

Blessed are the clean of heart,
for they will see God.

Blessed are the peacemakers,
for they will be called children of God.

Blessed are they who are persecuted for the sake
of righteousness,
for theirs is the kingdom of heaven.

Blessed are you when they insult you and
persecute you and utter every kind of evil
against you (falsely) because of me. Rejoice
and be glad, for your reward will be great in
heaven. (re: Matt 5: 3-12)

The Stations of the Cross

Kneel in front of the altar and say:

Jesus, you loved me so much that you died for my sins and rose again so I might share in eternal life with you, the Father and the Holy Spirit. May these Stations of the Cross help me to realize that love.

At each station, think about what happened to Jesus. Think about how he suffered for us and how much he loves us.

At each station say:
1 Our Father,
1 Hail Mary and
1 Glory to the Father

1st Station
Jesus is Condemned to Death

2nd Station
Jesus Takes up His Cross

3rd Station
Jesus falls the First Time

4th Station
Jesus Meets His Mother

5th Station
Simon of Cyrene Helps Jesus

6th Station
Veronica Wipes Jesus' Face

My Mass

7th Station
Jesus Falls a Second Time

8th Station
Jesus Meets the Sorrowing Women

9th Station
Jesus Falls the Third Time

10th Station
Jesus' Clothes are Torn From Him

11th Station
Jesus is Nailed to the Cross

12th Station
Jesus Dies on the Cross

13th Station
Jesus is Taken From the Cross

14th Station
Jesus is Laid in the Tomb

15th Station
Jesus Rises From the Dead

prayers... thoughts... sayings...

_____

_____

_____

_____

_____

_____

_____

_____

_____

_____

_____

_____

_____

_____

_____

prayers... thoughts... sayings...

_____
_____
_____
_____
_____
_____
_____
_____
_____
_____
_____
_____
_____
_____
_____
_____
_____

prayers... thoughts... sayings...

_____

_____

_____

_____

_____

_____

_____

_____

_____

_____

_____

_____

_____

_____

_____

_____

Prayer to My Guardian Angel

Angel of God, my guardian dear, to whom God's love commits me here. Ever this day be at my side, to light and guard, to rule and guide. Amen

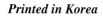

Printed in Korea